The Winning Partnership: CV and Job Applications

John Lowe

A Lowe Publication™

Text © John Lowe, 2011.

The right of John Lowe to be identified as author of this work has been asserted by him in accordance with the Copyright, Designs and Patents Act 1988.

All rights reserved. No part of this publication may be reproduced or transmitted in any form or by any means, electronic or mechanical, including photocopy, recording or any information storage and retrieval system, without permission in writing from the publisher.

Published in 2011 by:

**Lowe Publications
Linen Hall, 162 Regent Street
London, W1B 5TG
United Kingdom**

ISBN: 978-1-907824-04-3

Layout and illustrations by Giorgio Giussani.

Edited by Judi Hunter.

Printed in London by Empress Litho Ltd.

CV – How long should it be? One page, two pages or more? What should you put in and what must be left out? I have read over 100,000 CVs and have developed a simple template that always works. But a CV is never a standalone document. Discover the winning partnership!

Contents

About the author	**8**
Chapter 1 A successful CV and covering letter	**10**
Think context	12
Think audience	15
Chapter 2 CV composition	**20**
Use a narrative format	23
Two pages or longer?	24
CV example	27
Chapter 3 Responding to job advertisements	**32**
Recommendations	58
Conclusion	**60**

About the author

John Lowe, founding director of Regent Selection, Regent Coaching and Regent eLearning, is the author of *Your Lowe Profile* and one of the leading experts on career and personal development coaching.

John is a successful headhunter, recruitment consultant and coach and it is this rare combination of skills and his experience of having conducted over 20,000 interviews – all factors which collectively give him unique market and people insight. He personally coaches MBA students, university professors, Board directors and an extensive range of business executives.

The coaching always has a strong employability focus and John's first-hand knowledge of the market place is based on his expertise of conducting assignments with the world's largest corporations, SMEs and start-ups. Each industry and employment activity has its own dynamic and the structure and content of the coaching has been designed to embrace this divergence and variety. John has introduced an exciting new approach to conventional coaching through the identification and development of four distinct personality types. As the candidate recognises their type and individual strengths, they can then apply this knowledge to the critical employment stages of knowing what is their ideal job role, always successfully performing on interview and consistently enhancing a top performance at work. All these critical factors are described in the publication *Your Lowe Profile,* which can be used as an expert career coaching reference.

On a personal note, John is a graduate of the University of London where his Masters in Philosophy had a particularly contemporary focus on the role of ethics in our changing workplace.

This booklet highlights one of the key elements of the coaching programme: How to generate a really good CV and how to apply it when making job applications. Follow this method and your ratio of applications to interview will dramatically increase.

Chapter 1
A successful CV and covering letter

How to construct a good CV and covering letter is one of the most written about subjects in the area of career advice and coaching.

It is difficult for the reader to know what is correct advice. Clearly, the collective advice given cannot all be correct, as many of the books and articles on the subject contradict themselves. I shall introduce you to what I consider to be the ideal format from the employer's perspective. However, before I do, let's look at some common perceptions and misconceptions. This will encourage you to explore the real role of this summary description of yourself (Curriculum Vitae).

An analogy that candidates have found useful is to compare looking for a job with the search for a new car.

When you plan to purchase a car, you will have prequalified certain details and preferences: age, manufacturer, model, mileage, price range, colour, service history, condition, number of owners, and location for convenient viewing. The following advertisement will probably not create much enthusiasm.

> *Clean, well-maintained Ford Focus with low mileage. Reliable and regularly serviced. Must sell as owner is relocating abroad. Very competitive price and offers accepted.*

On the other hand, you may contact this owner for an exploratory conversation if it fits your criteria of price, etc:

> *Ford Focus ('06 model) Silver. One owner from new. Full service history. 18,000 miles. Showroom condition £6,000 ono. Oxford, city location...*

These comparisons, though exaggerated, make a salient point regarding the structure of your CV and why you must emphasise detail at all times. The pervading theme is to know that the reader is seeking factual information – not hyped generalisations.

Think context

I review many CVs with introductory mission statements:

A highly successful executive with a track record of achievement with excellent communication skills now seeking a challenging role to capitalise on a broad range of proven skills.

I do not give consideration to these statements – they give me no qualitative information. I need detail and facts and all statements must be contextually placed. Follow my CV format so that recruiters can make a fair assessment based on your real performance, not generalised, hyped narrative. Your CV will stand out from the crowd for its clarity, its ease of legibility, creating a positive attitude in the reader's mind.

You are, in fact, facilitating the recruiter to make a real and fair assessment of how well you match the vacancy – which will be composed of a factual, not hyped, description of duties and responsibilities.

Discussions that will ring a familiar note:

- ***How long** should a CV be?*
- ***How many** pages?*
- *Should I write a **mission statement**?*
- *People keep telling me to **mention my achievements**, but I can't really think of any big achievements – I just did the job!*
- ***Sell yourself** – but I am not a sales person…*
- ***Be brief.** The reader does not have much time! CVs are scanned first, not read in detail. But what does 'not much time' mean – 1 minute, 20 minutes?*
- *Put all your **details on one page** – if they require more information they will ask you for it! But my present CV is three pages – **which bits do I take out?***
- ***Use bullet points!***
- ***Mention your hobbies** so that the reader will have a better understanding of the real you!*

My advice is, without apology, directive and based on over 30 years experience of reading CVs and interviewing candidates for real live current vacancies and, because I am at the sharp end, I know at first hand what works and what does not. My experience spans all industries and services and includes some of the world's most prestigious recruitment projects. Each day I may review up to 100 CVs and I can pass on that experience to you to ensure that yours is in the selected category.

I have used this format when coaching main Board Directors of large corporations and when lecturing MBA students at leading universities from all world continents. The format is structured as a template that can embrace all skills of all employees from all industries including all nationalities.

So let us talk about CV writing and its format. Once compiled, it can be used for all applications. You do not have to generate a new CV for each job. The objective of the CV is to secure an interview for a suitable role, and I deliberately use the word 'suitable'. Its objective is not to overstate or distort your experience to gain an interview for a role in which you are neither interested nor competent to fulfil.

Think audience

Let us look at the situation from the recruiter's point of view. One of your staff has just handed in their notice and you need to replace them quickly. Or you have had a meeting with your colleagues and you have decided that, due to business expansion, you need to recruit a new person. You spend some time in drawing up a job description.

The job description will list the soft skills and technical skills required to carry out the role. The same will apply to the recruitment of the new candidate. Soft skills mean personality characteristics, for example determined, communicative, analytical, etc. Technical skills mean the candidate's ability and expertise in performing technical tasks, for example IT, accounting and marketing.

If your skills, as specified in your CV and in particular your technical skills, match the job requirement and your application is supported with an articulate email, then you will have an excellent chance of being called for an interview.

A further scenario: Imagine you are a company director who is seeking a candidate with two years experience of Apple Mac graphics packages to run and manage your design studio and you place the vacancy on your website. The ideal candidate will have a media or design-related degree. You receive an email from a candidate with four years Mac experience who has supervised a competitor's studio, has a degree in Product Design and lives five miles from your company's offices. You immediately respond to the candidate and invite them for an interview. The candidate applied at the right time and the details of their CV were clear. The recruiter was able to establish that there was a good match between their requirements and this candidate's skills.

If the next email you receive is from an accountant sent out speculatively, you will have no time to read it as you do not have a vacancy for an accountant. If, however, the next email is from another studio manager, I am sure you would read it avidly.

Exactly the same criterion applies to scanning a CV. I will only spend time on those CVs which match my job descriptions and, like the studio manager example, which I identify as a good match.

This means that 'mission statements' are irrelevant as they do not comply with the role for which you have sent your CV. Frequently, I have read mission statements, 'My career goal is to join a large multinational…' when the CV sent is in support of a role where the client employs 100 staff and is UK based! They can be read as being too non-relational and making exaggerated claims: 'Highly successful executive with a consistent track record of achievement and strong people management skills.' When I am reading a CV, I want facts that I can compare with a job description. 'Consistent track record' – doing what? 'People management skills' – how many and when?

Supportive statements can be included in your accompanying email where, from our examples, you can recognise how powerful and influential good contextual narrative can be in securing the interviews. Remember, I read CVs from a positive disposition and I am hoping that your CV matches the job profile – a fact that explodes the 'time' myth. You will read advice that employers will only have a few minutes to read your CV – you need something which will catch and hold their attention so you will have to sell yourself and produce a big mission statement or profile. Hopefully, I have discounted these claims. 'A CV should be no more than two pages' is another myth. If you are a university student with very little work experience, then two pages may be adequate. However, if you are a managing director of a £10bn multinational corporation employing in excess of 15,000 personnel, two pages will not allow you to elaborate your work experiences and skills adequately. A CV is primarily a factual information document, a summation of your experience to be compared with a job description.

The description should be clear, legible and factual. A CV then is a transparent, easily legible description of you and your experience presented in a positive and complimentary format.

This means your CV is:

- **easy to read – logical/transparent**
- **descriptive/informative – containing your personal and employment details**

- an account of your achievements and successes, always in a contextual format. What organisation did you work for, what did they do and when? Give details.

A CV works if it explains your personal details, education and work experience clearly, and if the recruiter has a vacancy that matches your skills.

A CV is always a contextual document. On its own, it serves no purpose. This point is important as much of the opinion concerned with CV writing is personally dovetailed as though the candidate were commissioning a painting or portrait of themselves. Try, then, to focus on the functional rather than the personal perspective of CV writing. Adopt the simple uncomplicated template in Chapter 2 and I shall tell you how to market your CV later. Let's get the composition right first. Remember, a CV is an easy-to-read description about yourself. It is, in fact, common sense.

Chapter 2
CV composition

A professional CV comprises two sections: a **main section** and a **supportive section**.

Part 1 Main section

Personal details

Name: Home telephone:
Address: Mobile:
                         Email address:
                         Nationality:

Education

University/college:
Location:
Dates: from/to:
Qualifications:

Education (continued)

School/college:

Location:

Dates: from/to:

Qualifications:

Employment history

Name of most recent employer:

Location:

Website:

Dates:

Description of employer:

Job title:

Duties and responsibilities:

Part 2 Support section

Addendum of projects

Project:

Client:

Description:

Your role:

Technical skills

IT skills:

Language skills:

Additional Information

Hobbies:

Interests:

Use a narrative format

The most effective CVs use a narrative format describing the work content and the candidate's involvement. This style is persuasive and has a positive influence on the recruiter. This transparency of content and the fluency of construction represent a successful and articulate candidate.

Commonly, candidates are advised to use bullet points for sentence construction and to ensure that the CV is no longer than two pages. This advice may sound good, but has no rational or authoritative foundation. I feel my reading skills are advanced enough to understand the significance of each word or sentence without it being highlighted by a repetitive bullet point. Don't use bullet points; use full descriptive sentences telling your positive story. This narrative format gives you the opportunity for more intelligent composition and chronological descriptions.

Two pages or longer?

The 'two pages' opinion also indicates a misunderstanding of the focus of the CV. If I was a Managing Director of a multibillion pound corporation being headhunted for a new role, I don't think the selection panel would be overly impressed with my two-page crammer. Clearly the number of pages will be determined by the nature of your previous role, your seniority and years of experience. A CV is read for its content, not its length.

If you are a consultant or architect where the nature of your technical expertise is determined by the nature of the projects you performed, which may include a variety of assignments, then you should list a sample of the projects separately, detailing their content, purpose and your role.

Similarly, IT executives will list their experience of applications, programming languages and hardware. Creative candidates with graphic design expertise should have a portfolio that supports their technical experience required for the role. The various projects, their content and your involvement can be separately listed under the title 'Addendum of projects'. This allows the recruiter to refer to the information if they consider it relevant and does not make the CV appear too elongated.

A description of your employer is important as it will contextually place all further details about you in terms of performance and responsibilities. Very often, I read a CV but cannot place the employer's activities and therefore cannot put the candidate's role fully into context. Certain roles may require previous industry-specific experience and it is important that the recruiter can identify the match. A short descriptive paragraph of your previous employers, their size in terms of turnover, number employed, product or service description and your particular division, role and activities, if relevant, is helpful to the reader.

You may also wish to give some additional personal information. This section is optional and will depend on the job for which you are applying and its relevance. It should include information that you think will enhance your application.

For example:

Gained the Duke of Edinburgh Gold Award.

Hobbies and sports: Captain College Hockey/Football Team.

Ran four half-marathons for charity.

I enjoy playing bridge and listening to music.

Be brief. Too long a list may give the impression that your hobbies or sport activities are your main focus, rather than your career.

CV example

Part 1 Main section

Personal details

David Rogers
70 Chalkson Street
London BR6 978

Home telephone: 020 974 4298
Mobile: 09676 412 981
Email: email@domain.com
Nationality: British

Education

London University
Regent Street, London
1999-2002
BA History 2:1

Ronan College
Mulberry Street, London
1992-1999
3 A levels (History Geography Biology)
9 O levels

Employment history

Barchester & Royce Ltd
Castle Street, Edinburgh
www.barchesterandroyce.com
June 2007 to present

Employment history (continued)

Barchester & Royce Ltd is a prestigious international group of management consultants. They concentrate on actively partnering large multinational corporates to formulate their global strategy. They employ approximately 6,000 consultants and have a turnover of £450m.

Marketing Manager

I manage a department of 10 staff and have overall responsibility for the £2m budget. I promote our brand using all the current social network media and I am tasked with managing all channels of online marketing, in particular SEO and SEM. I am responsible for the events team, which organises conferences, seminars, breakfast meetings and industry events to promote our brand and create new business. The board is keen that we identify new emerging markets with expansion potential.

My role is key as it is the link between the consultants and external stakeholders including clients, PR agencies and the mainstream media.

I ensure that our corporate policy is compliant with best sustainability practice and I have embedded these practices in our corporate mission statement and marketing campaigns.

My role requires a wide range of skills and has a direct and positive impact in generating new revenue. Innovation and embracing new technology is my forte and the board has acknowledged my key contribution through the 30% increase in my annual budget.

Backbone Ltd
Marshall Street., London
www.backboneltd.com
Sept 2002 to May 2007

Backbone Ltd is a small niche market research agency which helps its clients to stay ahead of their competition through quality research. The company employs 30 staff and has an £18m turnover.

Marketing Executive

My main responsibility was working as a research analyst on behalf of a broad portfolio of clients. My main activities included a range of activities in particular consulting, law, accounting, oil, construction and manufacturing.

I applied various quantitative and qualitative analytical techniques to their competitiveness, the corporate identity and the development of marketing strategy.

I personally presented actionable recommendations to our clients and was responsible for our 10 main accounts, which generated an annual revenue of £7m (for an example – see addendum section on the next page).

Part 2 Support section

Addendum of projects

UK leisurewear market

Large adult clotheswear retailer with 150 branches in the UK.

Budget: £400,000

Our client previously specialised in business wear for the 25–40 year age group. They wished to expand their business into other market segments beginning with youth leisurewear.

Using competitor data and observing the trends from the particular niche market leaders, and having conducted a product portfolio analysis, I commissioned two designers, who were at the cutting edge of British fashion, to produce samples for an exclusive trendy range which was bold in style and priced at the middle of the market.

I presented my recommendations to the Board incorporating strongly supported gap analysis and reports which were the outcome of comprehensive and complex qualitative and quantitative analysis. The Board accepted my recommendations and the initial launch was very successful and exceeded its target share by 40%.

The client has commissioned a further project with a budget of £600,000 to determine the best strategy to enter the adult market with a similar product range.

Technical skills

IT skills: Excel, PowerPoint, Adobe Illustrator

Language skills: French (conversational)

Additional information

CIM (obtained 2007)

Currently studying for an MBA

Chapter 3
Responding to job advertisements

Never send a CV on its own – you must explain the reason and context in which you are sending it.

You may be sending it in response to an advertisement and you must accompany the CV with a well-constructed email (or letter) outlining your reason for applying for the role.

A well-written email, outlining your suitability, will dramatically increase your chance of being called for interview.

An advertisement is a summary of a job description and will mention the salient skills required. When reading the advertisement, firstly identify the critical compulsory skills and construct your accompanying email in a way that demonstrates your expertise in that area.

I notice in your advertisement that you are seeking a candidate with analytical skills. In my current role, I research statistical reports and compile a summary…

Job descriptions, which are the source of information for the advertisement, will vary in length and detail. Some will be extremely cursory and brief. In some cases, the recruiter will not have a written job description but will work from a verbal briefing. In other cases, there will be a detailed and comprehensive description of the role. Terminology will vary but typically will include the purpose of the job, the description of the organisation, competencies and levels of experience, knowledge, qualifications, duties, responsibilities, activities, soft skills, technical skills, location and remuneration package. The description will specify and demarcate between essential required skills and those that are desirable but not critical.

When you are applying for a particular role, identify four skills requirements from the advertisement that you think strongly match your profile. Outline your relevant experience or competencies that endorse your suitability for the role. Your email should be specific and concise. Occasionally, some advertisements will invite you also to telephone to ascertain your initiative, often where good communication skills are critical to the role such as advertising, PR, business development and situations where you deliver client presentations. Make sure you do telephone. Use the content and format of your email as a guide for presenting yourself verbally.

Having submitted your application, you wait for a response. Don't expect an acknowledgement. Recruiters will not have the time to respond to each application and will often contact only those candidates whom they would like to call for interview. They may contact you by telephone or, more frequently, by email. Your job search is influenced by many unforeseen factors. The number of responses I receive will vary between 10 and 200 per role. Therefore, if a recruiter does not invite you for interview, it is often not that you don't have the experience and competency to carry out the role successfully, but merely that another candidate fits the criteria more closely in terms of location and competitor experience.

In your skills profile and CV construction you have identified your dominant competencies and you should only apply to roles that match those. Be selective; only make quality applications. Don't scan the job boards and apply to roles that look vaguely interesting with no regard for competencies required. Don't just click and send with the inevitable one or two-liner.

Please find enclosed my CV for the role of… If you require any further information, please email me or phone me on my mobile. I look forward to an early response.

This type of click and send normally promotes a click and delete.

Recruiters review applications from a positive perspective. They are hoping to find a match. As I am continually reviewing job descriptions, writing advertisements and managing responses daily, I know what works. Follow my advice in CV and email construction and you will dramatically increase your chances of being in that five per cent whom we are delighted to call for an interview.

Consider the following advertisements that I wrote and posted online when recruiting on behalf of prestigious clients. They were posted on leading job boards. You can then view real responses at first hand. This exercise will demonstrate the importance of formulating quality applications and dramatically increase your ratio of positive replies.

> **GRADUATE PUBLISHING**
> *LONDON*
> *£18,500*
>
> *This is an excellent opportunity for a graduate wishing to develop a career in publishing. Our client is a successful publisher of a range of magazines covering a wide subject area including Health, Auto, Music, Business, Property and Leisure.*
>
> *The successful candidate will spend time in various departments such as advertising, editorial, production, subscriptions and IT.*
>
> *The uniqueness of this role is the fact that the graduate will, after a year's introduction, have the opportunity to work in the department of their choice.*
>
> *Send your CV and an email outlining your reasons for applying to john.lowe@...*

This is an interesting exercise in terms of identifying the required key skills. The advertisement does not nominate competencies, but rather describes an opportunity for potential publishing graduates. Therefore, we can be assumptive and address the following key issues:

- Why are you choosing a career in publishing?
- Ambitious – explain and elaborate.
- Excellent communication skills are foundational to publishing, therefore the content and construction of your email will be judged in that context.

> *Dear John,*
>
> *I am particularly interested in your advertisement which offers a structured career in publishing. I have a degree in English and was the Editor of the University Student magazine with a circulation of 20,000. I regularly attend my local gym, play the guitar to Grade 7 standard and am a member of the local hockey team. I occasionally 'dabble' in stocks and shares. My wide interests replicate the breadth of your publications.*
>
> *I can attend an interview at short notice.*
>
> *Yours sincerely,*
>
> *A. Sample*

The response focuses exclusively on the role.

The candidate was **called for interview**.

> *Dear John,*
>
> *I enjoy writing and reading fiction. I enjoy current affairs and discussing topical events. Books are important in today's society when we watch so much television.*
>
> *Thank you for your time and I look forward to hearing from you.*
>
> *Best wishes,*
>
> *A. Sample*

Content and quality is poor and there is no engagement with the advertisement. **Deleted**.

> *Dear John,*
>
> *I have an honours degree in History from Durham and would like to apply for the Graduate role in publishing.*
>
> *I deliberately chose a literary subject and history in particular as, similar to publishing, it is conveying a message.*
>
> *I am an avid reader of a wide range of magazines and, in particular, Music and Health as they endorse my interests. I am a good mixer having established a wide range of friends at university and college and would*

> *(continued)*
>
> *enjoy the experience of interacting with the various departments.*
>
> *Publishing is my first career choice and I enclose my CV for your attention.*
>
> *Yours sincerely,*
>
> *A. Sample*

Good reply. Took care and time to write. The candidate was **called for interview**.

> *Dear John,*
>
> *I am attaching my CV for the job you are advertising.*
>
> *Yours,*
>
> *A. Sample*

Easy decision. **Deleted**.

> ***ECONOMIST/ANALYST***
> *WEST END*
> *£80,000*
>
> *This is an exciting new role with a prestigious investment institution where you will be responsible for economic analysis, statistical reporting, competitor analysis, creating working groups, organising and speaking at seminars, etc.*
>
> *The variety and scope are the most appealing elements, as well as the intellectual challenge and the opportunity for creative thinking in terms of best strategy and trends.*
>
> *Ideally, you will have a degree in economics and a further five years experience in a similar role.*
>
> *Telephone me, John Lowe, direct on…*

Four key attributes, therefore, that a suitable candidate for this Economist/Analyst role might possess could include:

- excellent analytical skills
- strong interpersonal skills
- flexibility
- creativity

We receive over 100 CVs with supportive emails everyday, some of which are replicated below. Judge which ones are the serious applications and the ones which you would consider to be the just 'click and send'.

> *Dear John,*
>
> *I am enclosing my CV for the online advertisement ref 61279428. I am going on holiday on Tuesday but can be contacted on my mobile even though I shall be in Cyprus.*
>
> *I am very interested in the job as I think it really suits me. So, if you have any queries, please call me even though I'm on holiday. I shall be back in the UK on Monday.*
>
> *Hope to hear from you,*
>
> *A. Sample*

What job is this applicant responding to? The reference number is the online advertiser's, not our reference. The respondent does not demonstrate any commitment or engagement with the role. **Deleted**.

Dear Sir/Madam,

I wish to apply for the position of Analyst because I think that I would be a suitable candidate. For this reason, please find attached my CV. If there is anything else needed in order to consider me, please let me know. Once you have had a look at my CV, if you are interested, I would be happy to discuss what I am doing now and my future aspirations.

Yours sincerely,

A. Sample

This example sounds polite, but it **does not engage** with the role and its responsibilities and the applicant is responding in a 'click and send' manner.

Dear John,

I am responding to your ad published online for an analyst. I enclose a copy of my CV for your attention.

I am currently working within the policy department of a prestigious merchant bank where I am supporting the

(continued)

department manager with economic and competitor analysis. I present my computations in the form of reports and, where the content is relevant, I take an active part in client seminars.

I have a Maths degree and enjoy the aspects that your advertisement is emphasising, particularly the intellectual and the challenge of combining my creative and statistical skills.

I shall look forward to hearing from you.

Yours sincerely,

A. Sample

Brief and to the point. An enthusiastic response – **I invited the candidate for interview**.

Dear John,

Please find enclosed my CV for the Economist job.

Thanks,

A. Sample

It is surprising how often I receive this type of response. **Deleted**.

DIRECTOR OF STRATEGY
RETAIL APPAREL or FMCG
LONDON

£75,000 + executive package

This is a challenging role in that it combines two critical skills – the ability to develop strategic plans and the ability to manage and implement the strategy.

The Director will be responsible for achieving volume targets for children's soft lines in the UK, which are marketed through licensees and retailers. You will be representing an organisation and brand that is a household name and carries a worldwide reputation for quality and innovation.

You will need excellent technical skills in consumer marketing, brand management, P&L, corporate business planning and global strategy. The ideal candidate will have a first degree and an MBA, with top-level negotiating skills and the flexibility to combine entrepreneurial drive with corporate objective.

You may prefer to discuss this exciting role with our Consultant on… prior to making a formal application.

We, again, highlight the dominant skills required:

- **Develop and implement strategic plans.**
- **Results orientated.**
- **Consumer marketing.**
- **Profit and loss.**
- **Negotiation.**
- **Initiative.**

Your email should include at least four skills that endorse your suitability for the role and match those specified in the advertisement.

Dear John,

The role of Director of Strategy appeals to me as it replicates my current role as Director of Communications with a large multiple retailer. I am responsible for the formulation of our global strategy throughout Europe and China and I supervise a team of 5 who are responsible for implementing the plans. I carry Profit and Loss responsibility of £20 million for my department.

I manage a sub division within my department, which is involved in brand and consumer marketing.

> *(continued)*
>
> *I have a BSc in Biology and an MBA from London.*
>
> *I enclose my CV and look forward to hearing back from you.*
>
> *Yours sincerely,*
> *A. Sample*

A strong, focused reply, which endorses a range of synergistic skills within brief, direct narrative. The candidate was enthusiastically **invited for interview**.

> *Dear Mr Lowe,*
>
> *I would be grateful if you would let me know if my application is successful for the Director of Strategy job.*
>
> *I have an MBA and I am looking for an executive position.*
>
> *Yours sincerely,*
>
> *A. Sample*

Not an engaging response. **Deleted**.

> *Dear John,*
>
> *Please find enclosed my CV for the Director of Strategy. You will see from my CV that I have been involved in global strategic planning and marketing for the Auto industry for 5 years. Previously, I was manager of strategy for a building products organisation specialising in interior products.*
>
> *I feel I have the experience you are looking for and look forward to your call.*
>
> *Yours sincerely,*
>
> *A. Sample*

Auto and interior products are technical experiences that do not match the job requirements. It would be better for the candidate to adopt a more selective approach at this level and seek roles that capitalise on their unique experiences. **Deleted**.

> *Dear John,*
>
> *I am hoping to find the opportunity to telephone you later today and, in the meantime, I would like to endorse my interest in your role for Director of Strategy – Retail. I have worked for an international retailer for the last 5 years where I am responsible for branding, product selection, sales and distribution of our entire apparel range, of which 30% is children's fashion.*
>
> *My previous 4 years was with a major food retailer where I had total European P&L responsibility for all ready-meal products. My experience of apparel, the retail market and ultimately P&L fits your dominant criteria of technical skills and I shall look forward to the opportunity of talking with you to define the people specification.*
>
> *Yours sincerely,*
>
> *A. Sample*

This is a strong response. The candidate has taken the time and care to engage with the advertisement.

A positive reply – the candidate was **invited for interview**.

REGIONAL MANAGER SOUTH EAST CONSTRUCTION EQUIPMENT
£60,000 + base

+ Up to 30% bonus + executive car and benefits

Leadership, initiative, teamwork, industry leading customer service, sound business strategy, profitable growth – these are the dominant factors that will be the hallmark of a successful Regional Manager.

This prestigious and high-profile organisation has a national and worldwide reputation for innovation, product quality and reliability. The extensive range of equipment includes excavators, loaders, dozers, rollers, dumpers, telehandlers, compactors and the applications will cover construction, quarrying, waste, demolition and material handling.

The Regional Manager's role could be described as the General Manager of the South East region as they will have the autonomy to apply their own skills in creative thinking, service delivery and leadership whilst being responsible for the P&L and all budgets.

The ideal candidate will have a track record of successfully managing a team of 50 plus and the technical experience gained in a similar or related environment. If you are very ambitious and seeking that ultimate challenge which packages all the exciting ingredients of world-class organisation, internationally known products, real career growth and dynamic management responsibilities, then telephone John Lowe in confidence on…

There is a wide range of experiences to choose from that are highlighted in this advertisement. Choose four.

- Leadership/management – 50 staff.
- Construction industry plant.
- Profit and loss.
- Business strategy.
- Customer focus.
- Performance orientated.
- Ambitious.

Dear John,

Further to our telephone conversation, I can confirm that I have 10 years experience within the mobile plant construction industry. I began my career as a Sales Executive and then joined the marketing department and, latterly, my role as a commercial manager incorporates P&L, recruitment and planning.

Consistently since my sales role I have exceeded all targets by 10% and I am now seeking a new challenge as stated in your advertisement.

> *(continued)*
>
> *I shall call you again on Tuesday to answer any questions you may have.*
>
> *Yours sincerely,*
>
> *A. Sample*

This is a strong response and, though brief, reactive in terms of the advertisement's specification. The candidate was **invited for interview**.

> *Dear John,*
>
> *I have been working in the construction industry for 25 years and know most of the major contractors. I have excellent management skills and in my present job I work under pressure whilst multi-tasking.*
>
> *Let me know if my application is successful.*
>
> *Yours sincerely,*
>
> *A. Sample*

This response is majoring on the 'construction' industry experience and ignores the rest of the criteria. **Deleted**.

> *Dear John,*
>
> *Your job for Regional Manager interests me as I am living in the South East. I have been with my present company for 8 years and I think it is time to move.*
>
> *You can call me on the mobile number on my CV.*
>
> *Yours sincerely,*
>
> *A. Sample*

Deleted!

MANAGING DIRECTOR EUROPE
MANAGEMENT CONSULTANCY
£400,000 + executive package

Our client is seeking an exceptional and insightful leader to manage new and exciting growth opportunities in the UK and Europe.

The dynamic change and short-termism that is prevalent in today's corporate environment is causing an onerous challenge to executives in terms of future planning and shareholders' expectations.

Our client advises medium to large international corporations on best strategic definition and implementation to manage and sustain performance improvement and growth. The Managing Director will have the support of a strong, competent Board, which is receptive to innovation and positive leadership. The ideal candidate will have exceptional skills in corporate management, strategic thinking, organisational planning and a successful track record of management within the service sector.

Our client has 15 offices throughout Europe and employs 3,000 staff. To apply for this role send your CV to John Lowe or, if you wish to find out more information, call John in confidence on…

We can identify the following skills as critical from the tone of the advertisement:

- Leadership – 3,000 staff.
- International experience.
- Planning.
- Determining strategy.
- Service sector.
- Performance orientation.
- Innovative.

> *Dear John,*
>
> *I am interested in applying for the Managing Director's role.*
>
> *I am currently the lead Consultant in a team of 500 where I am responsible for their performance and development. Our Consultancy is one of the world's leaders in global strategy and I am now seeking a new operational challenge where I can capitalise on my 15 years experience with my current organisation.*
>
> *Please let me know the recruitment process.*
>
> *Yours sincerely,*
>
> *A. Sample*

A good response. The candidate may not be logistically senior enough for the role in terms of people numbers and international exposure; however, they are **worth inviting for interview** as a candidate 'with potential' rather than proven track record. Personality and interview performance will be critical here.

Dear John,

I am applying for the position of MD.

I am working as a management consultant since being made redundant from my last job. I enjoy travel and in my present job I travel extensively.

You will see from my CV that I have the relevant experience and am used to managing people.

I am available immediately.

Yours sincerely,

A. Sample

This applicant does not engage with the critical content of the advertisement. Management consultants require good report writing skills and the respondent must therefore give a coherent account of themselves. **Deleted**.

Dear John,

I wish to formally apply for your MD role, Europe.

Fifteen years ago I commenced my career with a leading management consultant where I ultimately managed a department specialising in organisational change and development.

In my current role, I am the MD for a leading software house supplying technical integrated solutions to the publishing industry. My brief includes the UK and Europe.

I am responsible for setting strategy, identifying new markets and product innovation and ultimately corporate performance which has grown 20% year on year under my stewardship. We employ 2,400 staff in 7 countries.

I am interested in the role because of the new challenge it presents, capitalising on my management consulting expertise and combined with my successful track record of leading a prestigious organisation in a very competitive market. I enthusiastically wish to apply for the role and can be reached in confidence by email or on my direct number.

Yours sincerely,

A. Sample

A strong application endorsing the synergy of technical and soft skills and operational performance – the dominant criteria. The candidate was **invited for interview**.

> *Dear John,*
>
> *I am interested in applying for the position of European Managing Director.*
>
> *Could you please forward me a job description and application form?*
>
> *Yours sincerely,*
>
> *A. Sample*

No comment needed here. **Deleted**.

Recommendations

- Only apply for roles that really interest you and which match your skills.

- Don't send your CV speculatively in the hope that 'something will come up'.

- When you have identified a suitable role, spend time analysing the key skills required and then describe how they match your particular profile.

- Go for quality not for quantity.

- When you have constructed a really good CV you don't have to change it for each application – this is the point and role of the email or covering letter.

Conclusion

In my introduction, I referred to the diversity of advice on this well-covered subject: advice on content, style, bullet points, profiles, length and introductions. The frequent tone and focus of the advice is to make your CV striking, stand out, impress and wow the reader, leaving all the others in its wake, thus ensuring your CV goes to the 'top of the pile', winning on layout typography and eye-catching design. However, your CV is not a self-portrait to be viewed admiringly in its own frame. It is a functional, contextual document and part of the important process towards achieving your goal of securing the job.

Follow my directional and prescriptive advice and the happy conclusion will be compliant with the title of this booklet – you will have composed the perfect partnership, the winning CV and the winning covering letter.